The journey *to* wisdom

The journey *to* wisdom

Kate Hayes

The journey to wisdom

An individual or small group Bible resource from Scripture Union

Scripture Union, 207-209 Queensway, Bletchley, MK2 2EB, England, UK
Email: info@scriptureunion.org.uk
Website: www.scriptureunion.org.uk

© 2007 by Kate Hayes

ISBN: 978 1 84427 285 3

Scripture Union Australia
Locked Bag 2, Central Coast Business Centre, NSW 2252
www.su.org.au

First published in the U.K. by Scripture Union, 2007

Scripture taken from the New Living Translation, British text, published by Tyndale House Publishers, Inc., Wheaton, Illinois, USA, and distributed by STL Ltd., Carlisle, Cumbria, England.

British Library Cataloguing-in-Publication data
A catalogue record for this book is available from the British Library.

Cover design: Philip Grundy

Internal design and typesetting by Servis Filmsetting Ltd, Manchester

Printed in China by 1010 Printing International Limited

⚲ Scripture Union is an international Christian charity working with churches in more than 130 countries, providing resources to bring the good news about Jesus Christ to children, young people and families and to encourage them to develop spiritually through the Bible and prayer.
As well as our network of volunteers, staff and associates who run holidays, church-based events and school Christian groups, we produce a wide range of publications and support those who use our resources through training programmes.

The Way Ahead

W isdom perhaps seems an old fashioned kind of word, something we associate with the old or the long ago past. If you ask someone what characteristics they would like to exhibit, wisdom might not be top of the list. However, they might well say they would like to be successful. Throughout the generations people have had different ideas about what it means to be successful. Great minds have ruminated on whether a successful life is built on wealth, relationship, transforming achievement or power and recognition. Whatever a person believes about success, it rarely comes without effort. Even for those for whom money and celebrity seem to drop ready-formed from the sky, sustaining that lifestyle requires attention rather than recklessness, something we might like to call wisdom.

Eventually all success in life, however dramatic, has to face that well-known truth, 'you can't take it with you'. But is that really so? Maybe there is a way to 'take it with us'. God offers those who love and serve him, eternal life, a life beyond the grave. So perhaps we need to find out what God sees as success and, just as human success requires wisdom to sustain it, find the wisdom to sustain a life of success God's way.

Here, in this series, we focus on what it means to be successful in God's eyes. Finding sustained success means living wisely, according to his desires for us. So, how do we make wise decisions about life today? How does our desire to live life God's way affect the way we communicate with others and the way we relate to all those around them?

In everyday life, sustained success can be dependent on many factors, such as a good education, being in the right place at the right time, hard work and applying wisdom to life. The way we live day by day should be marking us out as followers of Jesus. Even so, our ultimate hope for the future, for eternal success, does not lie in our own hands. God's plan to bring his people into permanent and lasting relationship with him is built not on our efforts or our lifestyle but on Jesus himself, the one who not only shows us the way but *is* the way. Jesus isn't someone who offers us a way of life to follow but is the Creator and Sustainer of the universe; he is the source of life itself. We end by seeing that God's wisdom, God's plan for the world, is greater than anything we can come up with ourselves, Jesus is the only wise option for those seeking eternal success.

Whether you are reading this alone or as part of regular meetings with a small group, this book is for you. Where there are suggestions for activities that are

particularly suitable to be done alone or in a group, they're indicated with the
following logos:

The Solitary Traveller

This book is a companion for the solitary traveller. You can work through the
material at your own pace, ignoring only those sections marked with the group
logo. It may be helpful for you to record your thoughts along the way, either on
the pages or in a separate notebook.

The Group of Travellers

This book is also a companion for the small group. You may have come together
with a Christian friend, as a prayer triplet, as an existing small fellowship group
or you may be part of a group specially convened for Lent or some other season
of the year. Decide whether one person will lead each time you meet, or whether
a different person will lead each session. You may want to skip those sections
marked with the solitary traveller logo or allow people time for silent reflection.

Using the Material

The material is divided into six sessions or chapters and there is a consistent
pattern to the material in each.

Setting out will gently ease you into the focus of the session through some fun
questions or activities. Don't skip this part even if you are a solitary traveller,
because however light this material seems, it will flag up some important
attitudes and preconceptions and will prepare you for deeper exploration of
some key issues. Within the group setting, this opening time will develop
relationships and encourage honest sharing which will ultimately help the
group to be more comfortable in praying together.

Signposts will take you into the Bible. This time of discovery alone or together
will open up a number of lines of thought as you go through the questions. For
groups, this section will particularly encourage discussion and the sharing of
experiences.

Prayer is the next section, during which time there is opportunity to pray in a
way that relates to the focus of the session so far. Don't be tempted to rush this;
it is just as important as the rest of the session.

Further Afield is the final section. This allows further exploration of related issues in the Bible. Depending on how long you have together, groups wanting to lengthen the Bible study section could use some or all of this material in the SIGNPOSTS section. Otherwise group members might like to use FURTHER AFIELD at home for personal study during the week. Individuals can choose to use some or all of this section.

About the Author

Kate Hayes, born into a non-churchgoing family in Sheffield, decided to become a Christian aged 12 after being 'dragged along' to a Pathfinder meeting by a friend. After studying Psychology at university, she did teacher training but then found herself working in bookshops and in software testing for the book trade. Since 1994 she's been in Dukinfield, Greater Manchester, where she coordinates and writes materials for small groups at St John's Church.

1 Living a Successful Life

*W*hatever you think about the rights and wrongs of the Olympics coming to London, once the competition is underway there are going to be some new famous people around. Maybe they'll become well-known for their dramatic injury picked up in mid-competition, or for getting knocked out too early, or even perhaps for doing far better than anyone expected and ending up with a gold medal. Olympic success is a great achievement but what about success in other areas of life? Should we all be seeking some kind of success or is success something God wants us to be unconcerned about?

Setting Out

Imagine you are working for a newspaper. You've been given the task of running a Readers' Poll to find out who your readers believe are the three most successful people in the world today. Do you think the results would vary depending on which paper you worked for or do we all agree on who is successful?

Who do you think would be the contenders for that top three?

What about you? If your paper allowed you a vote, who would you choose?

Look at some magazines that cover celebrity lifestyles, and some national newspapers. If you are meeting as a group perhaps get everybody to bring a contribution.

What makes these people well-known?

Would you describe them as successful too? If so, in what way?

Did these papers and magazines mention the last person to serve you when you went shopping? Why do you think people in 'ordinary' jobs aren't usually covered by such magazines or the national newspapers?

Do you think someone has to be well-known to be considered truly successful?

Do you want to be successful?

Which of these would you most like to be able to say about your life? That it had:

- healthy, happy, rewarding relationships
- enough money to live on comfortably
- a place to live that you are glad to come home to
- interesting holidays
- work that is decently paid, challenging and benefits others

We would all prefer life to bring some kind of success. Are there things in the list that you would happily do without, that really don't matter to you?

Even though we all want to live successful lives, not everybody's ideas of what makes life successful are the same. Are there other things you would want to add to this list, things that demonstrate someone has lived a successful life?

Signposts

Read Ecclesiastes 9:11,12

Do you think it is true that someone can win a prize, get the best job or earn the most money when another person really deserved it more?

If so, why might that happen? Is it just down to being in the right place at the right time as the writer of Ecclesiastes suggests?

What about the successful people you considered earlier on, do you think they were just lucky?

Have you ever failed at something you really wanted to do well? How did it make you feel?

Whatever causes personal success it's certain that some people experience more of it than others. Even so, those who are successful at one thing may be hopeless at something else: the great footballer may be an uncaring and absent parent or the person who comes top of the class in French may not have a clue when it comes to Science. Equally, you may be stunned by a colleague's incompetence at work and yet find they are a tireless and loving carer for their elderly parents.

None of us wants to look at our lives and see failure, and yet sometimes that's just what we get. So, is it possible for us to be guaranteed a life marked by lasting success? Maybe! It depends entirely on what kind of success we are after.

Facing the challenge

Read Luke 12:16–21: The Rich Fool

Was the man wrong to spend time and energy on building a successful farm?

Why do you think God didn't commend him for his hard work and its
  successful outcome?

This man invests all his time and energy in building his farm to great effect, and yet Jesus says that wasn't the best use of those resources. We might expect Jesus to say the man should have spent more time on his relationships or on investing in his local community, but he doesn't.

Where did Jesus say the man went wrong?

Imagine someone has the idea for an invention that will end all the current and future damage of global warming. This is so important that they work 18 hour days for years on end, barely taking time to eat and sleep and certainly not spending it with God. Then just as the invention is finished, they die. Their death doesn't stop the invention from working, instead it will benefit others for generations to come and protect God's creation from disaster.

Do you think God would still describe this person as he did the farmer, as a
  fool? Why, or why not?

God sees success differently from most of us. Even if someone is an internationally renowned sports star, the greatest parent ever, a top-selling author, the pastor of a huge church or the fastest checkout operator in the land, for God none of that matters a jot if it means he is shut out of our lives. His first desire for his children is that they will come to him and follow him into eternity. In the end, any earthly success is just that; eternal success comes only from building our hearts and lives on Jesus.

Many people feel that they are too busy already. How could someone in that situation put God at the centre of their life?

What about you? Does your life have God at the centre or are your commitments pushing him out?

Can you see a time when things were different in the past? If so, what changed?

What could you do to put God first once more?

Living successfully

Read Hebrews 11:32–40

If you had put the people mentioned in this passage forward for your Readers' Poll, which ones do you think would have been chosen as successful?

What did the people in verses 32–34 achieve that might have impressed others?

You wouldn't find the people described in verses 35–38 on the front of many celebrity magazines and yet in God's eyes each of them was a great success. What kind of success did they experience?

Read 2 Chronicles 26

What made Uzziah such a successful King?

Do you think every success in life is a gift from God?

Eventually pride meant that Uzziah forgot his own sin and weakness and came to believe that he could achieve the same success without God. What might have stopped Uzziah falling into that trap?

For Uzziah, despite many years of faithful service, the consequences of his disobedience were severe. Do you think God took away Uzziah's power as retribution, or might there have been more to it than that?

In those years of isolation Uzziah had plenty of time to reflect on how things had turned out. If he had repented, what advice might he have passed on to his son (or even to us) do you think?

Finally

Just because earthly success doesn't last, it doesn't mean we can laze around doing as little as possible. Pleasing God comes from the way we live here on earth and we need his help to get that right. In God's wisdom we find his directions, his help, for life, something we'll explore in later sessions.

Prayer

Begin in silence, thinking about the great gifts God gives to us, things that bring us joy, encouragement and hope in life. Then pray single sentence prayers of thanksgiving, beginning with the words: 'Lord I want to thank you for. . .' Each prayer should include just one thing to be thankful for, but each person can pray more than once if they wish.

You might then like to choose a familiar song or hymn of worship, that you could sing or listen to that encourages us to express our thanks to God.

End by saying Psalm 111 together from whatever version you prefer. Try dividing into two groups with each group saying alternate lines.

Further Afield

1 SEEKING THE RIGHT KIND OF APPROVAL

Imagine you were going to meet someone for the first time and wanted to make a really good impression on them. What preparations might you make? How would you behave when you met?

How would you feel if after all your preparations this person decided they didn't like you at all?

When we want someone to like us we may be tempted to gloss over our bad habits. Maybe we'll allow a few untruths to bolster our image or go along with things we don't really agree with to keep them on our side. Seeking the approval of others can lead us onto dangerous ground.

Read 1 Thessalonians 2:1–4

How do you think Paul would have had to change his message for everyone to approve of him?

Paul didn't deliberately create dissension but he didn't worry about whether people liked what they heard either. For Paul, God's approval mattered far more than anyone else's.

We may not be great debaters but every moment of our lives is still a message to others about who we are and who we serve. Are there times when what you say or what you do is intended to keep in with people rather than keep you close to God?

Ask God to show you when you end up doing wrong things in order to win the approval of others.

2 FINISHING THE RACE

Do you enjoy sport? Whether you play it, watch it or hate it, you'll still hear about great sporting triumphs. The individual or the team will be headline news, there might be a parade in their hometown, there will be medals, prizes and fame. For most, that level of success will come rarely and it may well be the greatest moment of their sporting lives. Seeing such triumphs it can be easy to forget the preparation that led up to it. We don't remember those who drop out, only those who persevere right to the end.

Read 2 Chronicles 26:16–21

Have you ever started something new and then found your enthusiasm fading? What happened?

Why do you think that happens to us?

Uzziah started off well, serving the Lord and achieving great personal and public success but then he stopped too.

Read Philippians 3:12–14

The successful runner who stops training will soon stop winning. Uzziah stopped serving the Lord and his successes faded away. Paul reminds us that however well we are doing today, we still need to keep our focus on the finishing line, to keep on running right to the end of the race.

What warning signs might tell us we are in danger of giving up on the race?

What about you, are you still running strongly?

Spend some time in quiet, asking God to help you finish the race, whatever obstacles lie in your path.

3 TRUE SUCCESS

Read Philippians 2:5–11

Great success in life might bring someone a great deal of money, power and respect. They might be very influential and even have the ear of Presidents and Prime Ministers. Sometimes people pay to listen to their thoughts, watch their every move and aspire to be like them.

Philippians 2:6–8 describes the way Jesus lived on earth. Do you think this sounds like the life led by a successful man?

If not, how does it differ from the life you might expect a successful person to lead?

Even though Jesus' life wasn't full of the modern trappings of success, nobody else has had everyone on earth kneel before them, never mind every knee in heaven and every knee of everyone who has ever lived. Jesus lived an apparently unsuccessful life and yet is now raised to the heights of heaven, Lord of all.

Jesus models what it means to live a truly successful life, a model that is completely different from any we see around us here on earth. Spend some time reflecting on these words from Philippians. Thank Jesus for what he did for you, praise him for who he is now, and consider what it means for you to live like him.

2 Living Wisely, Living Well

ere you the kind of person who got asked to be the captain of the form or the sports team at school? Perhaps you're the last person any teacher would have chosen! Usually you have to have a responsible attitude and a lot of common sense to be in a such a position and that's not something every child possesses. Sometimes wisdom seems to be something we expect to find only in the old or the well-behaved, the adult version of those form captains. The reality is that God's wisdom is for everyone, and it isn't just about being good but it is something that will help us to live God's way, to live a successful life.

Setting Out

On a typical day which of these is most like you?

It's 7.30am and you're

- grumpily chewing on a piece of toast before heading out to work
- just finishing the ironing. You've also cleaned the kitchen floor, sorted the recycling bins and prepared the evening meal since you got up several hours ago
- asleep, and will be for some time yet
- at work
- rushing round sorting kids or pets or parents or washing or mess. . .

It's 10pm and you're

- sitting down to watch the news with a nightcap before heading off to bed
- already asleep
- just on your way out to meet your friends
- at work
- just starting to do a couple of hours decorating before bed
- heading for bed as soon as you've finished sorting those kids or pets or parents or washing or mess. . .

If you had an entirely free choice what time would you get up and go to bed?

Has that always been your preferred pattern?

Do you keep to it? If not, why?

Margaret Thatcher famously survived on about four hours sleep most nights when she was in office. In the end it became a habit and she couldn't really sleep longer anyway. Do you think you could cope with life on that amount of sleep, week in, week out?!

One of the most famous American citizens, Benjamin Franklin, writing in the 1700s, said, 'Early to bed and early to rise makes a man healthy, wealthy and wise'. Do you think there is any truth in that saying?

Research suggests that health and wealth are linked; the more wealth you have, the better the healthcare and the lifestyle you can buy. Do you think there is any way of guaranteeing ourselves health, wealth and wisdom?

It's pretty easy to see what the benefits of being healthy or wealthy might be but why might someone want to be wise?

Imagine everybody could guarantee having one of these things throughout life; health, wealth or wisdom, and take their chances with the other two. Which would you choose and why?

It seems nothing we do will guarantee lifelong health or wealth. The good news is that wisdom is different, it isn't something reserved for a few white-haired, highly knowledgeable individuals but is available to anyone. Even better if our living according to God's wisdom has eternal benefits.

Signposts

DEVELOPING WISDOM

Read Matthew 7:24–27

Wisdom comes from putting Jesus' teaching into practice. Even so, we won't experience a storm-free life. What does Jesus promise us?

How might living this way protect us from the worst of the storms of life?

Has being a follower of Jesus ever altered your approach to a stormy period in your life? If so, how?

LIVING NOT JUST LEARNING

In *The Message*, Eugene Peterson translates Matthew 7:24 like this: 'These words I speak to you are not incidental additions to your life, homeowner improvements to your standard of living. They are foundational words, words to build a life on. If you work these words into your life, you are like a smart carpenter who built his house on solid rock.'

Read James 1:22–25

Did you learn a foreign language at school? Were you best at speaking, reading or writing that language (if any of these at all!)? Why was that?

Can you now speak a foreign language reasonably well? Is that the same language you learnt at school or not? If not, how did you learn it?

Are there some people in the room who learnt a language at school but who can't really speak it with any fluency? Why might that be?

In a sense learning to live as God wants us to is a bit like learning a language. To be good at communicating with people in a different language you have to practise doing it. It doesn't matter how many lessons you've been to or even how long you've lived in that country, to communicate effectively day by day you have to try it out and keep on trying. In just the same way to live as God wants us to, to live wisely, we can't just learn what we should be doing, we also have to try and put that into practice every day.

In *The Message*, Eugene Peterson translates Matthew 7:26,27 like this: 'But if you just use my words in Bible studies and don't work them into your life, you are like a stupid carpenter who built his house on the sandy beach. When a storm rolled in and the waves came up, it collapsed like a house of cards.'

What do you think it means to 'just use [Jesus'] words in Bible studies'?

What could we do to encourage one another to work his words into our lives, not just talk about them?

CONSIDER

Once we know how God wants us to live, we are called to obey. Are there areas of your life which you know you are trying to keep God away from, areas where you are unwilling to change the way you live?

Sometimes we think we're doing pretty well at living God's way but maybe if we asked our church leaders or mature Christian friends they might want to suggest improvements in a particular area of our lives: the way we deal with anger, conflict or forgiveness; relationship issues; the way we spend our money, for example. Are you willing to ask someone what they think and then honestly consider what they say?

Why might someone else be able to see things about us and our lifestyle that we've missed?

What qualities should we look for in someone before choosing to ask them for their help?

Who do you know with those qualities that you could ask?

It can be a great challenge to live God's way. If you are having particular problems with an area of your life, maybe you could find someone to discuss it with. If you are meeting with a group, why not ask people to pray for you sharing only as much of your concerns as you feel able.

Prayer

Ask one person to read these words. You may want to allow short pauses during each paragraph, and then leave time for reflection at the end of each section (marked pause).Begin with a few moments of silence before you read.

Imagine you are outside in a powerful storm. It's completely black, not a trace of light in the sky. The wind is howling around you, trees are lashing against the nearby buildings and the gusts are so strong you find it hard to stand upright. Not only that, the rain is beating down around you and onto you and the puddles are rapidly deepening around your feet. Over the sound of the rain and the wind you hear the occasional rumble of thunder followed by the sky lighting up for a few moments.

(Pause)

Jesus said, 'Anyone who listens to my teaching and obeys me is wise, like a person who builds a house on solid rock. Though the rain comes in torrents and the floodwaters rise and the winds beat against that house, it won't collapse because it is built on rock'.

Are you listening to the words of Jesus? Do you seek them out, hearing them, learning them, obeying them? Is your life being built on the rock, the firm foundation of those words?

(Pause)

Then Jesus went on, 'Anyone who hears my teaching and ignores it is foolish, like a person who builds a house on sand. When the rains and the floods come and the winds beat against that house, it will fall with a mighty crash'.

Look back over the last day or two. Were there times you forgot those words of life and went your own way in what you said or thought or did? Maybe you were abrupt with someone who needed your time, or cut too many corners at work? Perhaps you gave into temptation? Or gossiped? Or neglected the opportunity to show care to someone?

(Pause)

There are times we all like to think about Jesus more than we like to put his teaching into practice.

Ask him to forgive you for those times now.

(Pause)

In Proverbs 3:1–6 it says, "My child, never forget the things I have taught you. Store my commands in your heart, for they will give you a long and satisfying life. Never let loyalty and kindness get away from you! Wear them like a necklace; write them deep within your heart. Then you will find favour with both God and people, and you will gain a good reputation. Trust in the LORD with all your heart; do not depend on your own understanding. Seek his will in all you do, and he will direct your paths."

If you want God to direct your paths in life, ask him to help you put his words into practice from now on. Consider if there is one particular thing you need to begin doing differently in future.

(Pause)

Repeat those final verses together to finish.

Some might also like to learn the words of Proverbs 3:5,6. If you meet as a group, you could agree that you will all try to learn the verses together, perhaps even having a small prize for everyone who can recite them (without cheating!) at another meeting.

Further Afield

1 WORDS TO BUILD A LIFE ON

Read Proverbs 2:1–22

Do you find it easy to ask for things you need? What about with God, is that different or not? We probably have many times when the last thing we feel is wise, and yet Solomon says that anyone can have more wisdom, just by asking God for it. Have you ever done that?

However, like most things, it's not quite that simple. Solomon also says that we must 'tune [our] ears', 'concentrate on understanding' and 'search' for insight and understanding (vs 2,4). Why do we have to work so hard at developing wisdom if it comes as God's gift to us?

But it's going to be worth it. What, does Solomon suggest, are the benefits of having wisdom?

Pray that God would give you greater wisdom. Spend a few moments reflecting on whether you work at developing wisdom, or just hope that it is somehow going to develop on its own. Pray that God would show you how to develop the wisdom you have in order to serve him more effectively.

2 MAKING AN EFFORT

Have you ever gone out of your way to go and speak to someone you thought of as a wise and knowledgeable person? Maybe you just prefer to speak to whoever you can find, who is handy at the time. Maybe you think such a wise person would be pretty scary, they might say things to you you didn't really want to hear. The Bible tells us of one person who travelled a long way just to spend time with someone who was truly wise.

Read 1 Kings 10:1–10 and Matthew 12:42

The Queen of Sheba must have had some wise people around her. Why then do you think she bothered to go and meet Solomon?

Do you think it was worth the trip? If so, how did it benefit her?

The people around Jesus had access to even greater wisdom and yet they often didn't listen to him. We too have easy access to his words and wisdom. Do you seek out those words as much as you could? If not, why? If you put aside a few more minutes each day to learn what the Bible has to say, what difference do you think it would make?

Sometimes reading God's Word just gets pushed out by busyness, and maybe then we need to plan our reading times more carefully. Maybe we need reminders as we might for other appointments, writing something on a post-it note, in a diary, or setting a reminder alarm, for example. If this is a problem for you, what could you do to plan your appointments with God from now on?

3 CHOOSE JESUS

Does eating 15 pounds of chocolate a year sound a lot to you? That's supposed to be the average amount eaten per person in the UK each year and, as more than 90% of us like chocolate, you may well be contributing your share! Even so, some other countries eat even more. The Swiss are reputed to eat 21 pounds each!

During Lent many Christians choose to give up chocolate or other indulgences. However that's not the only thing Christians do to mark Lent. Many choose to spend more time in practices that build their relationship with God, seeking him and his wisdom for their lives. Some arrange to spend more time alone, to pray, or study the Bible, and some choose to fast. Others may read a book that encourages them to think more about their relationship with Jesus or with his world and some to reach out and get involved through some kind of extra service for those in need.

Do you wonder how you could possibly fit anything else into your life? Read these words to remind us how precious God's word and presence is.

Read Proverbs 8:10,11

What extra activity or time could you give to building your relationship with God and his people this Lent?

And if it's not Lent, don't be put off! Giving extra time to getting to know God better, to serving his people or learning more about him isn't going to be wasted whatever time of year it is.

Spend some time in prayer now. Try not to ask God for things, but instead to be quiet, just enjoying his presence with you today.

3 Living Wisely: the way we make choices & decisions

*D*o you prefer coffee to tea? Chips to new potatoes? Broccoli to sprouts? Choices constantly come at us from every direction. Some are about relatively insignificant things and others about life-changing issues such as our relationships and jobs. But how do we decide? Who says which choices are the right ones and which are wrong? Just how do we make our decisions about the way we live?

Setting Out

You come home from a long day out, tired and hungry, and find yourself in a very untidy house.

Do you

- scream and shout (whether that's at your family, the cleaner, the lodger, yourself, the cat. . .)
- sigh and get on with the cleaning before you do anything else
- ignore the mess until after food, then spend the evening sorting it out because you can't relax if it's not tidy
- ignore the mess, it'll wait till you feel stronger
- make someone else (cleaner, lodger, family, cat. . .) sort it out. You didn't do it, so you're not tidying it
- think that just wouldn't ever happen to you

Are you the kind of person who easily ignores household mess?

And do you create significant amounts of it?

Was that true of you at 14? Did your bedroom fit the stereotype of untidy teenagers?

What makes you tidy up (if anything at all!)?

Even a simple task such as tidying requires us to make a choice. We weigh up the pros and cons, our personal preferences, the expectations and wishes of others and make that call. For some of us even our mother, the Vicar or the Queen coming to tea isn't enough to get us tidying, our motivation still isn't strong enough. For others it's almost that mess equals meltdown, it must be got rid of before anything else can be dealt with. Some people can go to bed leaving the last week's washing up in the sink, others can't believe that it's physically possible to sleep when any household task is unfinished.

The truth is that every choice, every decision we make is motivated by something.

Signposts

MAKING WISE CHOICES

Read Acts 5:1–11

Ananias and Sapphira faced a choice; they could tell the truth to the apostles or they could deceive them.

Why do you think they made the choice they did?

Do you think Sapphira would have changed her answer if she had known what happened earlier?

For most of us knowing how things would turn out would make decisions a whole lot easier. We'd know whether that job would work out, whether pursuing a relationship with that person would turn out to be a waste of time, whether moving to rural Italy would make life less stressful or see us slinking home a few months later broke and miserable. Sometimes the idea that someone could tell us exactly what to do seems like a great idea!

Where might someone (Christian or not) go for advice over a life-changing decision?

How do you decide which sources of advice are most worth exploring? What makes some sources more useful to us than others?

Even when we seek advice, we still have to decide whether to take it or not. For Christians, there is one ultimate source of direction and that's God himself. And yet. . . it's still rarely that simple. Since becoming a Christian have you ever faced a big decision and not known what God wanted you to do?

Even if we know we want to do what God wants us to do it can be hard to work out just what that is. So often we still have to make decisions without any obvious direction from God, spelt out in huge letters in the sky. Here are four things that will help us make choices and decisions God's way, the wise way.

1 DOES IT FIT IN WITH GOD'S WORD?

Have people ever made assumptions about you, perhaps that you wouldn't understand something or didn't know how a thing worked? Perhaps their assumptions were about you as a person, your personality or interests or family life?
If that has happened to you, how did you feel?

Why do you think this can happen?

What about you – have you ever made an assumption about someone that got you into trouble in some way?

We don't just make assumptions about people, but also about other areas of life too. It's quite possible that we've made assumptions over what living God's way really means. Perhaps we've only half understood something, maybe we haven't considered that something we do is not really what God wants for us. We need to find out the truth about what it means to live life God's way.

Read Proverbs 1:2–5 and 2 Timothy 3:16

When did you last find God's word made a difference in the way you chose to act in a particular situation?

Whether our decision is a big one or an apparently trivial one, we need to check it out with what God has already told us about the way we should live.

2 IS GOD LEADING ME IN A PARTICULAR DIRECTION?

Read John 10:3,4

Someone rings you up and doesn't give you their name (and you don't have any kind of caller identification either!). What affects your ability to identify them?

Here the sheep recognise the gatekeeper's voice because he's so familiar to them they can pick him out and follow him even in a crowd. If we want God to lead us, then like the sheep, we need to be able to recognise his voice. We all have many voices competing for our attention including our own desires, the expectations of family or friends or employers, and the commitments we've made. All these things can affect us and make it hard to pick out God's voice.

How do you think we can learn to hear God's voice amongst so many voices?

Spending time in prayer is a great way to learn to recognise God's voice, but we're still not likely to hear him speak aloud. Have you ever had God speak to you during a time of prayer?

How did you know it was God?

Our feelings can give us clues to a particular direction to go in, but the best guide is God himself. The better we know him, the easier it is to hear his voice and choose according to his desires for us.

3 WHAT DO OTHERS THINK?

Have you ever made a decision and then later realised that it was a daft thing to do? Sometimes that was perfectly obvious to those around us and seeking their advice could have saved us from ourselves.

Read Proverbs 12:26, 13:14 and 19:20

What are the benefits of getting advice from others?

Have you ever received advice that was either excellent or disastrous? What lay behind such success or failure do you think?

Imagine you're concerned about your health. Would you seek advice from a random passer by in the street? Why?

When we're making decisions that affect our lives, it's crucial to choose our advisors carefully. What qualities should we be looking for in someone we plan to approach?

What if we don't have anyone around us we could approach; are there other sources of advice and wisdom we could tap into?

If we choose our guides wisely, they can offer us a different perspective on our situation, a perspective that may help us clarify what to do or not to do in a particular situation.

4 UNTIL TOLD OTHERWISE

Read Matthew 28:19,20 and Mark 12:28–31

Some people, such as Jeremiah, Moses and Paul, were clearly called to do a specific task for God. Many others were not and yet they were still God's people, living for a purpose. Jesus spelt out his summary of what every person who follows him is called to do. Unless told more specifically, this is our calling in life, this is what God made us to do. Bearing our ultimate calling in mind can be another source of help as we face choices in life.

Sometimes none of these things seem very helpful. We may face a big decision and find no clear direction from these sources. What do you think someone should do then?

Finally

Have you ever bought something that has a lifetime guarantee? Did you ever make use of it?

Do such guarantees tempt you into a purchase? Why?

Read Proverbs 3:5–7 and John 5:24

The best guarantees available on earth guarantee something for a lifetime, maybe several lifetimes. When we make the wise decision to live life God's way then we know that his guarantees, his promises to us, are not limited by our lifetimes. Instead, they last for all eternity.

Prayer

Have one person read the introductory sentence in bold and then read the words of Psalm 33 together. Follow each reading with a time of either open or silent prayer on that section's theme.

A Creator God

The psalm calls us to praise the Lord for who he is, his power and his love.

Let the godly sing with joy to the Lord, for it is fitting to praise him. Praise the Lord with melodies on the lyre; make music for him on the ten-stringed harp. Sing new songs of praise to him; play skilfully on the harp and sing with joy. For the word of the Lord holds true, and everything he does is worthy of our trust. He loves whatever is just and good, and his unfailing love fills the earth. The Lord merely spoke, and the heavens were created. He breathed the word, and all the stars were born. He gave the sea its boundaries and locked the oceans in vast reservoirs. Let everyone in the world fear the Lord, and let everyone stand in awe of him. For when he spoke, the world began! It appeared at his command.

Pause for prayer

A God we can rely on

The psalm reminds us that although he is our all-powerful Creator, God isn't distant and untouchable but is constantly watching over us, his people. Nothing we make, nothing we do can guarantee us a safe passage through life. Only God has that power, only his plans can never be knocked off course. We can put ourselves in his hands and know that he can be trusted to bring us safely through life.

The Lord shatters the plans of the nations and thwarts all their schemes. But the Lord's plans stand firm for ever; his intentions can never be shaken. What joy for the nation whose God is the Lord, whose people he has chosen for his own. The Lord looks down from heaven and sees the whole human race. From his throne he observes all who live on the earth. He made their hearts, so he understands everything they do. The best-equipped army cannot save a king, nor is great strength enough to save a warrior. Don't count on your warhorse to give you victory—for all its strength, it cannot save you. But the Lord watches over those who fear him, those who rely on his unfailing love. He rescues them from death and keeps them alive in times of famine.

Pause for prayer

A God who guides his people

Give thanks for God's constant and reliable presence in your life. Thank him for the times you have heard his voice guide you in making a wise choice. Give thanks for those who encourage you to follow his direction in life.

We depend on the Lord alone to save us. Only he can help us, protecting us like a shield. In him our hearts rejoice, for we are trusting in his holy name. Let your unfailing love surround us, Lord, for our hope is in you alone.

Pause for prayer

Finish by sharing prayer requests for any situation where you or those close to you, don't know what to do next and need to know God's direction. There may also be situations where you do know exactly what to do next but lack the courage to get on and do it. Share as much or as little of the detail as you feel able and then end by praying together for these things.

Further Afield

1 WHOSE EXPECTATIONS?

Read Luke 10:30–37

Have you ever been in a situation where a particular kind of behaviour was expected? Did you live up to those expectations or do you see that as a challenge to do exactly the opposite?

Jesus told this story about people who didn't live up to expectations. The one who did the right thing, didn't behave as everybody else expected, but as God expected him to.

What expectations do you think other people have of you? What expectations do you have of yourself?

Do you think those expectations fit in with what God wants for you?

Spend some time considering whose expectations control your choices and decisions in life. If it isn't God, be willing to ask him what changes he might want you to make from now on.

2 GOOD SENSE

The 'brainy but scatty professor' is a stereotype, but have you ever come across someone who really was highly intelligent but completely hopeless at coping with the ordinary demands of daily life, someone who seemed to lack common sense?

It's not just the bright who can lack that practical side to them. Sometimes Christians fall into a similar trap, but they often rely on sounding 'spiritual' when common sense is needed instead.

Read Matthew 10:5–16

It's not that we shouldn't be praying and relying totally on Jesus in every situation but that part of doing that is using the common sense God has given to us. Here Jesus reminds his people that they should be 'as wary as snakes', wisely applying common sense to their dealings with the world. Our times are potentially no less difficult for us and we need to approach our daily life with a healthy dose of common sense alongside our prayers.

Ask God to help you discern when a situation requires nothing more than an application of common sense and when something else is needed too. Ask him to show you if there is something you are involved with now where common sense has been missing and its return would help things move forward.

3 DISTRACTIONS

Have you ever been out to buy one particular item and come back with something completely different? Why do we sometimes get sidetracked in this way?

Shopping isn't the only place where we can get distracted. We forget that task that needed doing, to call back that person, to bring the washing in, the appointment, to take along that item we promised to lend a friend. . . Fortunately, forgetting to do most of these things are only an inconvenience, but as Christians we can also get distracted from our walk with Jesus, a distraction that is much more than being inconvenienced.

Read Proverbs 4:25–27

What kind of things do you think can distract us from following Jesus as we should?

Are you conscious of things that are distracting you from building your relationship with Jesus? Or things keeping you away from serving him as he wants you to? Or from living a lifestyle that honours him?

Think about these different areas of your life, and ask God to show you if he is concerned about any of them. You might also want to run the question past a trusted friend.

If there are problem areas, decide what you could do to get back on track, to living the life that God has called you to.

4 Living Wisely: the way we speak

❛ Sticks and stones may break my bones, but words will never hurt me'. A familiar phrase but one we might all want to disagree with and to change. The Bible has strong words reserved for the damage the tongue can do. James says it is 'an uncontrollable evil, full of deadly poison', Proverbs says it can cut like a sharp razor. Have you ever found yourself going back to something said to you that made you feel good, dwelling on those words again and again? Words can kill or nourish life, says Proverbs 18:21. But what about us? Do our words bring death or life to those we meet?

Setting Out

Six different means of communicating: phone, email, face to face, post, text, instant messaging. Which of these would you choose (you can use each more than once) to:

- say 'thank you' for a present from your distant aunt
- resolve a disagreement with a friend
- argue your case for a pay rise
- find out whether your neighbour's daughter passed their driving test today
- check what time your meeting starts
- catch up with someone you haven't seen for ages

Why did you make the choices you did?

Are there some of these that you never use, and others you really like? Why?

If you were only allowed to use one of these ways to communicate, which would it be?

Are you naturally talkative? Or are you the strong, silent type?

What do you think are the benefits of being chatty?

And quiet?

And are there downsides of these too?

Signposts

Read Proverbs 10:19 and 17:27,28 and James 1:19

This doesn't sound like good news for the chatty! Why do you think these verses suggest that only speaking a little is a good thing?

Does this mean that someone who says very little is less sinful than someone who talks a lot?

Read Proverbs 18:20,21 and Matthew 12:36,37

So perhaps its not really how much we speak but what we say when we do speak. Our speech can bring life or destruction, both to ourselves and to others – and so living wisely, living God's way means being responsible for what we say. What kinds of speech should we aim for, and what should we avoid?

Proverbs 18:4 says, 'A person's words can be life-giving water; words of true wisdom are as refreshing as a bubbling brook'.

Three ways to make our speech life-giving

1 KEEP CONFIDENCES

Read Psalm 41:6, Proverbs 11:13; 16:28; 18:8

How does gossip damage our relationships?

Why do you think people like to gossip?

Proverbs 26:20 says, 'Fire goes out for lack of fuel, and quarrels disappear when gossip stops'. It can be easy to find yourself being drawn into gossip. Are there situations where you find yourself vulnerable to this?

How could someone who doesn't want to gossip avoid getting drawn into a gossip session?

Is it ever acceptable to say something negative about someone when they aren't there?

Proverbs 25:19 says, 'Putting confidence in an unreliable person is like chewing with a toothache or walking on a broken foot'. Gossip causes great pain to others. Can you be trusted to keep confidences?

2 DISAGREE WITHOUT BEING DISAGREEABLE

Do you ever enjoy arguing?

What makes an argument a negative experience?

Another word for a destructive argument is a quarrel.

Read Proverbs 12:18; 13:10; 15:1 and 2 Timothy 2:24

What damaging ways of speaking and relating to one another are described in these verses?

Imagine the government was going to pass a law banning three phrases commonly used in quarrels in the hope of reducing the frequency of quarrelling in society. What three phrases do you think might be chosen?

Why are these words so provocative or damaging?

It can be hard to be patient, gentle and kind when we really want to scream and shout. How could someone avoid getting into a quarrel even though they are under stress and very upset?

Proverbs 18:19 reminds us that 'it's harder to make amends with an offended friend than to capture a fortified city. Arguments separate friends like a gate locked with iron bars'.

How can we disagree constructively with someone who isn't going to like being disagreed with?

3 ENCOURAGE ONE ANOTHER

Read Proverbs 11:9; 12:18; 27:9; 27:17

Have you ever stayed awake chewing over something someone has said to you that upset you or hurt you in some way? Maybe you can remember hurtful things said to you many years ago, even in childhood. Why do you think words can take root in our heads in this way?

Imagine you've been told you're to go on a rigorous exercise programme for medical reasons. To help with this, one of your friends, family and colleagues may either:

A. Remind you regularly that you should be exercising, offer you leaflets for sporty activities, and give you a hard time when you forget or can't face doing any.

Or

B. Offer to join in your exercise programme, come with you to the gym after work, get up to join you on your early morning run, call to see if you want to join them on a day out walking.

How would you feel if those around you were using option A?

And option B?

Actions can affect how we feel, and words can too. Words can make people feel small, belittled and a failure or they can make people feel encouraged, understood and that there is hope for the future. However, words don't always come out positively unless we make the decision to speak to people that way.

Are there people around you (family, friends, colleagues, neighbours, etc) where much of your speech to them and about them is negative and critical?

What do you think are the dangers of speaking to someone or about someone this way?

How could we make the way we speak to someone more positive, even when we don't like the way that they behave?

Do you think speaking positively to someone means overlooking their problems or failings?

What about someone who is clearly off the rails, living a sinful life and needing correction? Is it possible to speak to such a person positively?

Some people seem to enjoy finding fault with others, picking out their failings and criticising them. How can we encourage people like this to be more positive and encouraging in the way they deal with others?

Finally

Read James 1:26; 3:2–12

Why is the way we speak such an important indicator of the reality, or not, of our faith?

The person who is becoming wise in God's eyes, is someone who is learning to control their speech. We need God to point out our failings and then be willing to change. James also says that those who can control their tongues can control themselves in other ways too. We've probably all spoken those snappy, irritated words that reveal exhaustion or impatience. But what about day by day? What kind of person do your words reflect you to be? What do they say about what is really going on inside you?

Commit yourself over the next week or so to listening to your own words. Ask yourself:

What do they say about you?

What impact do they have on those that hear them?

What good or bad patterns can you see in your speech?

Perhaps you could also ask a trusted friend to tell you if there are things about your speech you need to work on.

Prayer

We may or may not be good at encouraging one another but there is one unfailing source of encouragement open to us. God's words are always ones of truth and hope. Even when we are facing difficult truths about ourselves, there is hope to be found in the reminders of God's love and his promises to us when we seek to obey him.

Have someone read slowly through these verses of encouragement and hope. Allow time for reflection after each one.

How precious is your unfailing love, O God! All humanity finds shelter in the shadow of your wings. Psalm 36:7

He prayed, "O Lord, God of Israel, there is no God like you in all of heaven or earth. You keep your promises and show unfailing love to all who obey you and are eager to do your will." 1 Kings 8:23

Jesus Christ is the same yesterday, today, and for ever. Hebrews 13:8

"I command you—be strong and courageous! Do not be afraid or discouraged. For the Lord your God is with you wherever you go." Joshua 1:9

Use these words to lead into your own prayers of thanksgiving for the enduring love and care God shows to his people, and to you in particular.

You could follow this by giving thanks for those who encourage you and for those known to you who need encouragement at present.

Is there some way you could be a part of the answer to those prayers by offering encouragement to someone yourself?

If you're not very sure what to do, discuss together the things that might be an encouragement to someone in need, then choose one or more that you think you could offer the people you prayed for today.

Further Afield

1 BE TRANSFORMED

Read Matthew 12:33–37

When did you last say something to someone that you shouldn't have said? Why do you think you said those words?

Sometimes when we're angry, stressed, or upset, negative words just come out, it's almost as if we can't help it. In a calmer state we'd have had more patience and they'd have stayed unsaid, maybe even unthought. And yet Jesus makes it clear that it's not just when we're under pressure that our words reflect our feelings. Every word we say says something about our inner selves, our attitudes and feelings, good and bad. If that's the case, then cleaning up our speech isn't just about trying harder, but about seeing the way we think and feel come to reflect Jesus more closely so that change makes a difference in the way we speak as well. Ultimately that change only comes through the power of the Holy Spirit working in our lives.

Reflect on the way you have spoken to those around you over the last day or two: include those close to you, those you work with, those you've spoken to in passing, perhaps in a shop or on the street. Ask God to show you if there were wrong attitudes behind some of the things you said, or the way you spoke to those people. Do you need to ask someone to forgive you?

Romans 12:2 says, 'Don't copy the behaviour and customs of this world, but let God transform you into a new person by changing the way you think. Then you will know what God wants you to do, and you will know how good and pleasing and perfect his will really is'.

End by asking God to change the way you think so it reflects his attitudes towards the world and his people, so that change will be seen by others in the words you say.

2 GOD'S WORDS OF POWER

Do you like making things? Imagine you decide to make a cake. You go into the kitchen and stand in the middle of the room reading the recipe out aloud. Once you've finished reading through it you look around the room. Do you see the finished cake? Why?

Read Genesis 1:1–31

God wanted to make something, but his words are so powerful that he didn't need to do anything but speak things into existence. His words are truly words of life.

Use the words you read in Genesis to consider what God's words reveal about him and his character. You might like to continue in prayers of praise, focussing on the power and majesty of God, revealed in his creation.

3 GOD'S WORDS OF TRUTH

From Simon Schama to Adam Hart-Davis and from Battlefield Britain to the World at War, history plays a significant part in TV scheduling. Do you enjoy such programmes? If you could travel back and visit one era in history, which would it be?

A famous comment says that 'we learn nothing from history except that we learn nothing from history'; in other words, we just keep on making the same mistakes. Do you think that is true?

Read Hebrews 4:12

Just as we can learn our history and still fail to apply its lessons to today, so too we can read the Bible and fail to realise that it is not merely describing events and people of long ago, but has a message for you and me today. Here the author of Hebrews reminds us that God's Word tells us more than who God is, it also tells us who we are. When we allow his word to speak into our lives, it lights up the truth about our real selves.

How often do you think you read the Bible and fail to really consider what difference those words need to make in your life? When you read God's Word, take your chance to learn the lessons of history and allow it to reach into the present to transform you.

5 Living Wisely: getting along with people

*H*ow many friends do you have? People assess friendship differently. Some include their friendly acquaintances, people they share lifts with or trust to feed the cat and water the plants when they're away. Our family may be our closest friends or they may be the people we least want to be with out of everyone on the planet! Some friends may be lifelong, others may come and go as circumstances change. Some may even end up as our enemies. Whatever we think of as friendship, however strong all our relationships, getting along with people is rarely simple.

Setting Out

Do you like Christmas? What is best or worst about it for you?

Do you think Christmas cards are:
- a waste of time and money and should be banned
- an opportunity to exchange news with distant friends and family
- a way of showing everyone you know that you're thinking of them and/or thankful for them
- a chance to brighten up the house and make it look festive
- a vital indication of your personal popularity
- a boring chore that you always seem to leave beyond the last possible minute

How many Christmas cards do you send out each year?

Is it possible to still be friends with someone when your only contact is an annual Christmas card?

Signposts

Fred and Tom are constantly rubbing each other up the wrong way and they think the other person is really difficult to get on with. However, they also both have good friends whose company they enjoy and who find them easy to be with.

Why do you think we find some people easy to get on with and not others?

Unless we become hermits, we can't completely avoid those we find difficult. In reality most of us probably find even those (or especially those) closest to us difficult and annoying at times. Jesus said, 'I command you to love each other' (John 15:17), but that can be hard to do. For example:

1 IMPERFECTIONS

Wanda is your good friend; loyal, funny and caring but she's also the kind of person who borrows things and never returns them, promises to meet you somewhere and then doesn't turn up, and has a robust line of embarrassing jokes with you as the subject. Sometimes you cope perfectly well with all this, but how might it make you feel if it happened too often, or if you were having a bad day?

Eventually you decide you're going to have to challenge Wanda about these annoyances. Frustratingly, she just isn't really sorry, saying she doesn't mean anything and it's just the way she is. We have limited time and energy to give to our friendships, so would it be best to avoid Wanda from now on?

Read Proverbs 17:9, 19:11 and Galatians 5:15

Do you see yourself as someone who can be critical of others or do you disregard people's failings?

Are there some faults that are too great to be overlooked?

Why might we choose to overlook the failings of others? (You might find Ephesians 4:31,32 helpful).

What are the dangers of focusing on people's failings?

Why might it be worth investing time and energy into an imperfect friend?

2 THE COST

Read Proverbs 11:25, 2 Corinthians 9:6–8 and Philemon 1:6

Giving isn't just about money, but, for example, also about possessions, time and energy.

What should power our desire to be generous towards others?

Which of these things do you think you find easiest to share with others? And hardest? Why is that?

Sometimes the demands and needs of those close to us can leave us feeling weary and overburdened. Do such feelings justify putting our need for rest or peace above their needs?

When the demands on us are high, we need to find ways of being refreshed and restored ourselves. What kind of things help to bring this about?

What about you, what helps you to feel refreshed and renewed?

Do you usually make the effort to do these things before life overwhelms you or do you keep going till you burn out?

What about the present time? Are you taking enough time for rest and renewal or not?

Why it matters

Jesus describes the true mark of a good relationship, saying, 'And here is how to measure it – the greatest love is shown when people lay down their lives for their friends' (John 15:13). We are called to love others sacrificially. But why is it so important?

Read John 13:35

How can the quality of our relationships, inside or outside the church family, show non-Christians that we follow Jesus?

Do you think the relationships between people in your church are significantly different from those between non-Christians?

What are the strengths of relationships within your church? And weaknesses? How could you improve those weak areas?

What about you – does the way you run your relationships make a positive impact for Jesus?

The hardest thing

It isn't always easy to care for those who are important to us and are committed to, but it gets harder still. . .

In relationships, as in everything, Jesus is our model. His relationship with us is not about what he can get out of it but exists solely because he loves us – something that endures however we behave in return. (You might like to look at Romans 5:6–8 here).

Read Proverbs 24:17, Matthew 5:38–48

As Christians, the problems of learning to love others are not restricted to loving those we like. We're to love even those who hurt us or those who aren't remotely interested in our well-being.

A work colleague is constantly sniping at you. They take pleasure in trying to make you look silly or incompetent in front of others, they're disrupting your relationships with your colleagues, and they're even apparently trying to get you into real trouble, demoted or sacked.

Have you ever been in a workplace where that was happening?

If this was happening to you, would you most like to:

- see one of your colleagues behave towards them as they are to you but with greater success
- rise above the situation and ignore them, meanwhile hoping everyone else will see their malicious spirit and take your side
- rally an army and smite them from the face of the earth
- file claims of bullying against them with your employers

- sit tight and just hope that they leave before you disintegrate
- go off sick

Which of these options do you think would qualify as 'loving your enemies'?

Read Proverbs 25:21,22 and Romans 12:17–21

How do these verses suggest we should deal with people who are out to harm us?

What do you think that would mean in dealing with that impossible colleague?

What if they don't appear to be shamed when we return their hatred with love? What happens then?

Do you think it is necessary to feel kind and forgiving towards someone before attempting to build a positive relationship with them?

Imagine you have made the effort to overcome your natural inclination to hurt this person in turn. Instead you pray for them, offer them a friendly greeting on your arrival at work, include them when you brew up and even ask how their day went. All you get in reply is more problems. What now?

Are there still possible benefits to you from doing this or is it all a waste of time?

Do you think that there are some situations when we can justify avoiding a person who has hurt us?

If so, is there anything left we can still do to improve that relationship?

Have you ever tried to build a relationship with someone who was an enemy, or at least someone you found extremely difficult? If so, what happened? What advice would you give to someone who wanted to do the same?

Is there a relationship in your life that you need to attend to, whether that's with someone you love or someone you don't? Decide on the first one or two steps you are going to take and when you will do them. You could share some of the details with a trusted person and ask them to pray for you and support you in this.

Prayer

The words in bold come from Romans 12:9–18.

Have one person lead the prayer by reading those passages and everyone responds with the words in light type. After two sections you may want to stop and encourage people to pray for individuals and you may also want to allow time for prayer or reflection at the end of each section. Decide before you start whether people are to pray aloud or in silence, with the leader continuing after an appropriate interval.

Don't just pretend that you love others. Really love them. Hate what is wrong. Stand on the side of the good. Love each other with genuine affection, and take delight in honouring each other.

Lord, there are people in my life who I love and want to thank you for now.

[Pause to pray for these people.]

Even so, there are also many I don't find so easy to love. Help me to live a life that is marked by love even when I don't feel like it, when people are difficult, demanding and annoying and when they don't express love to me in return. Your love for me is undeserved and never fails, help me to share that same love with others too.

Never be lazy in your work, but serve the Lord enthusiastically. Be glad for all God is planning for you. Be patient in trouble, and always be prayerful. When God's children are in need, be the one to help them out. And get into the habit of inviting guests home for dinner or, if they need lodging, for the night.

Father, forgive me for the times I have overlooked those in need around me, out of fear and selfishness and when I hope or expect that someone else will come to their rescue. Everything I have in life is a gift from you; alert me to the needs around me so I may wisely and willingly share those gifts with others to bless them as you have blessed me.

If people persecute you because you are a Christian, don't curse them; pray that God will bless them.

Lord you love all your children, those who follow you and those who stand against you. You long to be welcomed into every life so you can bring transformation and new life to us all. Just as we pray for those we love, we pray for all those who don't know you, even those who are persecuting your people, here and around the world. May your love and life take root and flourish in them so that one day they will be changed into your witnesses, people who share your good news so that others come to know you.

When others are happy, be happy with them. If they are sad, share their sorrow.

Lord we want to thank you for all those we know who are celebrating at the moment.

[You may want to pray for particular people and events known to you here.]

We also remember all those who are sad and pray that they will experience your strength and hope at this difficult time. [Again you may want to pray for particular people and needs here.]

Live in harmony with each other. Don't try to act important, but enjoy the company of ordinary people. And don't think you know it all! Never pay back evil for evil to anyone. Do things in such a way that everyone can see you are honourable. Do your part to live in peace with everyone, as much as possible.

Lord, there are things about the way I relate to others that need to change. Show me how you want to work in me, and help me have the courage and the wisdom to follow your call. May I become so like Jesus that his light shines in me and through me into the lives of all I meet.

Further Afield

1 I'M NOT WITH THEM

Do your friends or family ever embarrass you? Do you think you ever embarrass them? In extreme cases we may even want to pretend we're not really with the person involved, we try to look just as puzzled or upset by the behaviour of this supposed stranger as everybody else around us.

Read Matthew 26:57–75

Peter denied knowing Jesus but it wasn't out of embarrassment. Why did he pretend he didn't know Jesus?

Have you ever been scared to admit you knew someone? Have you ever been scared to admit you knew Jesus?

Jesus was being beaten nearby and Peter had no idea how those around him would respond if he admitted his connection to Jesus. Following Jesus can be scary and costly, although for us it's rarely as risky as it seemed to Peter that day. Pray now for those who face just this kind of challenge every day in other countries around the world, from neighbours, colleagues, governments, even their family and friends.

2 FOR BETTER OR FOR WORSE?

From tempting us into that extra piece of cake to encouraging us to go to the gym, our friends make a difference to us. Teenagers often hang around as part of a big group of friends. Was that true for you? If so, were those people always a 'good influence' on you or not? Being with a group leads many people into doing things they'd never do on their own, and that can be a good thing but is also often the reverse.

Read Proverbs 2:20, 13:20 and 27:17

Do you think it is possible to have a significant relationship with anyone and not be shaped or changed by it?

Think about those you spend time with at present. Do you think they have a good influence over you?

What kind of influence do you have over them? Are you good for them?

 Spend a few moments reflecting on your relationships.

Do you spend enough time with those who are positive influences on you?

What about those who lead you away from Jesus? Do you need to avoid them or can you stay friends without allowing them a negative influence over you?

Give thanks for all these people, for their presence in your life. Ask God to help you be someone who shines the light of Jesus into their lives.

3 CLOSE TO HOME

Sadly church relationships don't always demonstrate Christ-like attitudes; bitterness, jealousy, anger and resentment appear here too.

Read Colossians 3:14,15 and 1 Peter 3:8–12

Do these words sum up the relationships in your church at present?

What about your own relationships with others in your church? Be honest. Is there someone you find difficult and can't truly say you are at peace with? If so, how could you do something about this? The Bible calls us to be willing to make the first move.

Spend some time praying for the relationships between people in your church, for the positives and the difficulties. Give thanks for the peacemakers in your community and those who model the loving attitudes these verses describe.

Ask God to show you how you can demonstrate his love towards his people more effectively in the future.

6 Ultimate Wisdom

Wisdom is no absolute guarantee of being right. Over the centuries many wise scientists and researchers have sought answers to complicated questions. In the end they've found answers that seemed certain and true to everyone and a 'fact' was born. Then, one day, new evidence came to light that proved that 'fact' was completely wrong. It wasn't that those people were bad at their job but that some vital piece of evidence was missing for some reason, maybe, for example, because the technology they needed to find it hadn't been invented. Those people were the wisest of their day and came to the best conclusions they could with the evidence before them and yet they were wrong. The best of human minds is limited and can take us in the wrong direction.

Starting Out

What's the best April fool joke you've ever come across?

Do you ever take part in April fool jokes today? What do you think of the tradition?

Do you think you are easily tricked into believing a hoax or getting caught out by a joke?

Once some beliefs were widely held but aren't any more, believing that the earth is flat, for example.

Why don't you believe that the earth is flat?

Imagine if one of our leading politicians happened to mention in an interview on the Radio 4 breakfast programme Today or on Newsnight with Jeremy Paxman that they seriously believed the earth was flat. How do you think the interviewer would respond?

Do you think holding that kind of belief would alter the way they were seen by the general public? Why?

Signposts

1 FOOLISH IDEAS

Read 1 Corinthians 1:18–24

In verses 22 and 23 Paul says, 'God's way seems foolish to the Jews because they want a sign from heaven to prove it is true. And it is foolish to the Greeks because they believe only what agrees with their own wisdom. So when we preach that Christ was crucified, the Jews are offended and the Gentiles say it's all nonsense'.

Do you think people today still think that being a Christian is foolish?

Why didn't people want to believe in the Christian message in Paul's day?

Do you think people have similar reasons for discounting it now? What kind of reasons have you come across for people not being willing to believe in Jesus?

How might you answer someone who said they needed absolute proof that Jesus really existed and rose again?

Or the person who thinks that no rational person could believe in the supernatural in our modern world?

Or someone who says, 'I tried praying for the end of world poverty or for protection from the effects of a natural disaster and it didn't happen, so I don't believe in God'?

People have all kinds of reasons for discounting the Christian message and yet Paul reminds us that we shouldn't be surprised by that. We need to recognise that our message does sound strange, that people will think it is foolish and that many will treat it in the same way as they would the belief that the earth is flat.

Why do you think God chose to reconcile people to him in a way that was against all expectations, all human ideas of what is right and sensible to believe?

2 AND THE WISEST OF PLANS

Read 1 Corinthians 1:25–31

What do you think is the greatest invention ever?

And what one invention would you love someone to come up with?

There are some great inventions around. Even so, our greatest ideas and our greatest inventions still come from limited human minds and the biggest concerns of our world remain unsolved. We still have a world where people die every day from a lack of food, clean water and basic medical care. We still go to war with one another, and ultimately we all still die. Human ideas and understanding can be amazing and yet they don't have all the answers our world needs.

The Message translates verse 21 like this: '[Since] the world in all its fancy wisdom never had a clue when it came to knowing God. . .'

Not only does human wisdom fail to sort out the problems of the world, it also fails to make any real progress towards knowing God. Most of those who met Jesus in person still missed the truth of who he was and that saw him crucified, the man who was God himself (2:8,9). Our only lasting hope lies in trusting in God's wisdom, in his understanding and his power.

Few people don't want to be successful in life. We've seen through this series that true, lasting success does not flow from human ideas and human wisdom, as every human eventually comes to the grave. We've also seen that God's wisdom offers us a path to eternal success and that if we are serious about seeking that success we will want to live life his way. However, the end of our journey does not come about from our own efforts, living a 'good life' isn't the guarantee of eternal life.

Politics, the environment, music and healthy living are just some of the different things that can become a focus of someone's life.

Have you ever been sufficiently interested in one of these things for it to affect your lifestyle?

Why do you think some people make one of these things the whole focus and purpose of their life?

For some, being a Christian, a follower of Jesus, is similar to having a passion like these and it affects their whole lifestyle, leading them into a new way of life. And yet, following Jesus is more than another lifestyle choice. Jesus does not just offer us something to sign up to, a way of life to follow, he offers us himself.

Read Colossians 1:15–20

The ultimate sign of wisdom is not the decision to take on the new lifestyle associated with 'Christianity'. The ultimate wisdom is God's plan to reconcile us to him through Jesus, the Creator and Sustainer of the universe. If we want to be truly wise, then we need to seek Jesus and build a relationship with him. Our behaviour, our lifestyle changes come in response to that, flowing from our desire to know, to please and to serve him.

3 BEING WISE

So, if we want to be wise with a wisdom that is greater than anything found on earth, anything that depends on the limits of the human mind and heart, we need to seek Jesus before everything else.

Read Matthew 13:44–46

Do you think these men were taking a risk when they sold all they had for the treasure or the pearl?

Why might some people think they were foolish?

And others see it as wise?

If we react to Jesus as these men did to the treasure and the pearl, is that a risk?

How do those around you, amongst your family, friends, colleagues, and neighbours feel about you making such a decision?

How do you feel about living and working alongside those who think you are, at best, foolish?

Read Matthew 6:9–13 and Luke 17:20,21

Where does Jesus say God's kingdom is to be found?

The Lord's Prayer includes the words, 'Your kingdom come'. What do you think those words mean?

The impact of sin on our world is so great that God's kingdom is not yet fully realised here on earth. Even so, he has many kingdom-builders in residence whose qualifications are that they recognise him as their Lord and King and seek to serve him. Those people, those kingdom-builders are you and me, God's foothold in his world.

4 LIVING FOR THE KING

Read Matthew 5:13–16

Mix salt into your cooking and it will add flavour to the whole pot. Turn on a light up high in a room and it fills the whole area around it. We are called to make an impact not just on others who follow Jesus, but on all God's people – including those who think we are fools. To represent Jesus we need his wisdom, the understanding of what it means to live God's way, and the willingness to put it into practice whatever the cost.

Over these sessions we've looked at the need to accept the King's definition of success, success that comes in loving, knowing and serving him. We've also looked at how God's wisdom will make an impact on the way we make decisions, in the things we say and in our relationships.

Which of these sessions did you find most interesting or most helpful? Why?

If you were going to take away just one thing from this series, one message or idea what would it be?

And what is the most important thing you are going to do differently as a result of this series?

As we allow our lives to be directed by God's wisdom, we will become more and more like Jesus. As that happens, the more effectively we will shine his light and his love into the lives of all his children, including the many who don't yet know him.

Prayer

As you have done in previous sessions, have one person read the words in bold (taken from Luke 23 & 24), and then all read the words in light type as a prayer together. Allow time after each section either for personal reflection on that theme, or for further prayer together.

Two others, both criminals, were led out to be executed with him. Finally, they came to a place called The Skull. All three were crucified there—Jesus on the centre cross, and the two criminals on either side. Jesus said, "Father, forgive these people, because they don't know what they are doing." And the soldiers gambled for his clothes by throwing dice. The crowd watched, and the leaders laughed and scoffed.

Lord, Jesus was abandoned on the cross by almost all those who he had shared his life with. They left him and hid, afraid to be caught and to suffer alongside him. It's easy to see that those who took part that day and those who ran and abandoned Jesus needed your forgiveness, and yet they aren't alone. My sin also pinned him to that cross and left him there. I'm sorry for all those things I have done wrong and for all those things I didn't do when I should have done, forgive me too, Lord.

[Pause]

"He saved others," they said, "let him save himself if he is really God's Chosen One, the Messiah." The soldiers mocked him, too, by offering him a drink of sour wine. They called out to him, "If you are the King of the Jews, save yourself!" A signboard was nailed to the cross above him with these words: "This is the King of the Jews." One of the criminals hanging beside him scoffed, "So you're the Messiah, are you? Prove it by saving yourself—and us, too, while you're at it!" But the other criminal protested, "Don't you fear God even when you

are dying? We deserve to die for our evil deeds, but this man hasn't done anything wrong." Then he said, "Jesus, remember me when you come into your Kingdom." And Jesus replied, "I assure you, today you will be with me in paradise."

Lord, from that day people have believed that the cross was a defeat, and death was the end for Jesus. Yet Jesus promised the criminal that he would be with him in paradise. On the cross, death became victory, its power destroyed. Lord, I choose to follow you along the path that leads from death to life.

[Pause]

But very early on Sunday morning the women came to the tomb, taking the spices they had prepared. They found that the stone covering the entrance had been rolled aside. So they went in, but they couldn't find the body of the Lord Jesus. They were puzzled, trying to think what could have happened to it. Suddenly, two men appeared to them, clothed in dazzling robes. The women were terrified and bowed low before them. Then the men asked, "Why are you looking in a tomb for someone who is alive? He isn't here! He has risen from the dead!"

Lord, you have given us the task of sharing the good news that Jesus is alive. Teach me to speak his words of hope and life to all your children. Teach me to love them as he loves me. Help me to seek out and follow your direction, your wisdom for my life that I might become more and more like Jesus, salt and light in your world.

[Final pause]

Further Afield

1 REFLECTING HIS GLORY

Do you enjoy watching adverts? What's the best advert you've ever seen?

One problem for advertisers is getting the balance right between making an attractive advert people take notice of and making it so interesting that you remember the story but completely forget what it is trying to advertise.

Read 2 Cor. 3:18–4:2

As Christians in some ways we are 'adverts' for Jesus. We aren't adverts in the sense of talking of the good things about following him and ignoring the cost, or pretending we now live perfect and problem-free lives. Instead the way we are day by day communicates something about Jesus to others. So often people's attitudes to the Church or to Christians define their attitudes to Jesus himself. If they don't like us, they think they don't want to know him either. If we want them to see the real Jesus, we need to live as he wants us to, reflecting his glory more and more.

Reflect on the messages your life gives to others about Jesus. As sinful people we aren't ever going to give others an unblemished picture of Jesus, but do you still give people glimpses of the real Jesus or not? What needs to change in you to make the message clearer?

2 THE LAST WORD

When you argue with people do you need to have the last word? Are you someone who just has to get that parting shot in before the subject is closed or can you bite your tongue and allow the conversation to end with someone else in charge? Even when we know we're wrong, getting the last word can make us feel we've regained a little bit of power or control in a difficult situation. Deliberately allowing someone else to have the last word can be a challenge!

Read Hebrews 8:10

It may not be easy to give someone else the last word, and yet if we choose to follow Jesus, that's just what we are doing, choosing to let someone else have the final say in our lives. We let go of our own preferences and trust that God's way is really the best, a path that will lead us to truth, to purpose, to belonging and to eternal life.

End by reading and praying through these words from Psalm 25:4–10:

Show me the path where I should walk, O Lord; point out the right road for me to follow. Lead me by your truth and teach me, for you are the God who saves me. All day long I put my hope in you. Remember, O Lord, your unfailing love and compassion, which you have shown from long ages past. Forgive the rebellious sins of my youth; look instead through the eyes of your unfailing love, for you are merciful, O Lord.

The Lord is good and does what is right; he shows the proper path to those who go astray. He leads the humble in what is right, teaching them his way. The Lord leads with unfailing love and faithfulness all those who keep his covenant and obey his decrees.

3 KEEP YOUR EYES ON HIM

Read Colossians 3:16,17

Whether we are a leader or a follower, someone who loved school or hated it, someone who has been a Christian for years or for days, greater wisdom is available to us all. 'Let the words of Christ, in all their richness, live in your hearts and make you wise', says Paul. If we commit time to reading our Bible and acting on what we learn, to prayer, silence and reflection, we will become wiser than we are today.

Put aside some time today to read God's Word and pray. Ask God to give you wisdom, a greater understanding of life from his point of view. Listen for what he wants to say to you and be ready for him to work in you to change you so that you become more like Jesus.

End by reading these words from Romans 16:25–27:

God is able to make you strong, just as the Good News says. It is the message about Jesus Christ and his plan for you Gentiles, a plan kept secret from the beginning of time. But now as the prophets foretold and as the eternal God has commanded, this message is made known to all Gentiles everywhere, so that they might believe and obey Christ. To God, who alone is wise, be the glory for ever through Jesus Christ. Amen.

OTHER TITLES by KATE HAYES

A Journey of the Heart: a pilgrim's guide to prayer

A companion to this book, with identical format. If you want to explore what it means to pray with purpose, growing in understanding of and intimacy with your God, this series of six Bible-based studies – which can be tackled in a small group or on your own – will take you on a rewarding journey. 48pp
ISBN 1 85999 797 X

The Journey of the Son

The second in this series of studies. Based on Matthew's portrayal of Jesus' road to the cross, these six studies consider the struggles we also face to do God's will. We see how Jesus coped with temptation and emotional turmoil, and stayed the course to the end. 56pp
ISBN 1 84427 097 1

A Journey of Discovery: on the road with Jesus' followers

Kate Hayes invites us to dig deeper into Luke's portrayal of how the first disciples grew in their understanding of Jesus and what it meant to be his disciples. What should be our priorities as we seek to live God's way? How can we cope with pressure and failure? 64pp
ISBN 1 84427 180 3

A Journey of Love: reaching out as Jesus did

Throughout his life Jesus was guided by a clear sense of mission. We too are called to reach out in love as Jesus did. Kate Hayes invites us to think about what it meant for Jesus to be sent by his Father and what it means for us to follow Jesus' example today. 64pp
ISBN: 978 1 84427 232 7

All suitable for individual or group use, at Lent or any other time.

THE RE:ACTION SERIES – 6 SMALL GROUP RESOURCES (all 48pp)

For the tough times
Does God care when I'm hurting?

Whether it's thousands killed in a terrorist attack as you watch on TV, your next door neighbour on chemo for cancer, or your best friend's marriage on shaky ground ... there's no escaping the issue of suffering. Maybe you want to shout at God that's it's just so unfair! Just what's it all for?
ISBN 1 85999 622 1

Chosen for change
Am I part of God's big plan?

Like it or not, you're living in the 'me' culture. Are you comfortable with going t alone, taking care of 'Number One', cashing in on 'your rights' and turning a blind eye to responsibilities? What about sharing… caring… belonging… teamwork… community? Are you ready to serve not self – but society?

ISBN 1 85999 623 X

Available from all good Christian bookshops or from Scripture Union Mail Order: PO Box 5148, Milton Keynes MLO, MK2 2YX, tel: 0845 0706006 or online through www.scriptureunion.org.uk

SCRIPTURE UNION
USING THE BIBLE TO INSPIRE CHILDREN, YOUNG PEOPLE AND ADULTS TO KNOW GOD